MUSIC AND LYRICS
BY
COLE PORTER

A Treasury of Cole Porter

with an Introduction by Robert Kimball

CHAPPELL & CO., INC.
NEW YORK

RANDOM HOUSE
NEW YORK

PHOTO CREDITS:

P. 2, 5, 6, 7, 8, 9, 158: Various Cole Porter Collections
P. 4: Original pencil drawing by Lorelle Raboni
P. 15, 150: MUSEUM OF THE CITY OF NEW YORK (Theatre and Music Collection)
P. 28, 120, 278: CULVER PICTURES, INC.
P. 33, 37, 71, 111, 178: VAN DAMN PHOTOS, Theatre Collection, The New York
                         Public Library; Astor, Lenox and Tilden Foundations
P. 96, 169: THEATRE COLLECTION, The New York Public Library; Astor, Lenox
            and Tilden Foundations
P. 266: Courtesy of Gretchen Wyler
P. 288: Camera Portrait by Phyfe

A special debt of gratitude is expressed to Robert Kimball
for his valued assistance in the preparation of this book and
to Irving Brown and Mary Ellen Stamford of Warner Bros. Music
for their co-operation and help.

ISBN 394-70794-X
Library of Congress Catalog Card Number 72-3980   Book Designed and Edited by LEE SNIDER

CONTENTS

COLE PORTER

by ROBERT KIMBALL

This book is a tribute to Cole Porter, one of America's foremost song writers. A courageous man and a great artist, Cole Porter wrote glorious music and sophisticated lyrics that splendidly evoke the times in which he lived yet have endured to bring pleasure to millions and to become a significant part of our cultural heritage. Witty, urbane, ebullient, and poignant, the best Porter songs are crafted with skill, beauty and intensity of expression that bear the subtle and unique qualities of artistic genius.

Here is the most comprehensive collection of Cole Porter songs ever published. Here, too, are the complete lyrics of many songs presented with their music for the first time in the form that most closely approximates Cole Porter's original intentions.

Born in Peru, Indiana on June 9, 1891, Cole Porter was the son of Kate Cole and Samuel Fenwick Porter. He received his formal education at Worcester Academy (1905-09), Yale College (1909-13), Harvard Law and Music Schools (1913-16), and the Schola Cantorum in Paris (1920-21). His musical education, one of the most extensive ever received by an American theatre composer, began under his mother's tutelage with the study of piano and violin. Cole's earliest attempts at composition produced such precocious, albeit pedestrian, concoctions as the *Song of the Birds* (1900) and *The Bob-O-Link Waltz* (1902). His appetite for lyric writing was whetted by his father's avid interest in classic languages and nineteenth century romantic poetry, interests that were further developed in prep school and college.

Linda and Cole on board the Chonsu

In June, 1917 he sailed for Europe to work with the Duryea Relief Organization but within a few months enlisted in the French Foreign Legion. Later in the War he was attached to the American Embassy in Paris, where on January 30, 1918, at a wedding breakfast in the Ritz Hotel for Ethel Harriman and Henry Russell, he met the exquisite Linda Lee Thomas. Linda, an elegant divorcée whom Bernard Berenson succinctly described as "a great beauty with great brains" and Cole fell in love and were married in Paris in December, 1919.

John Wilson, Noel Coward, and Cole (Venice)

It was at Yale that he first found his niche as a song writer, creating the famous football songs *Bull Dog* and *Bingo Eli Yale*. His Yale Glee Club specialties (displaying a burgeoning kinship for the lofty heights of the Keith vaudeville circuit) and the musical comedy scores he wrote for his fraternity Delta Kappa Epsilon's initiation plays and the Yale Dramatic Association have been fondly recalled by his contemporaries for their suave, audacious lyrics and captivating music that already forecast the attributes of Cole's later distinction.

Although his Yale triumphs had earmarked him for almost certain success in the theatre, his Broadway debut as the composer and co-lyricist of the comic opera *SEE AMERICA FIRST* in March, 1916 was a fiasco that lasted for only fifteen performances. (Porter had vainly sought to be the American "Gilbert & Sullivan.")

Cole Porter on the Lido in Venice (1920's)

Venice: Cole with friends. Note Fanny Brice (seated on left) and Elsa Maxwell (seated, 2nd from left)

For a substantial portion of the 1920's Cole and Linda Porter made Europe their home, especially Paris and Venice. They travelled widely and lived and entertained on a grand scale. Linda widened Cole's artistic horizons by introducing him to many outstanding cultural figures as well as leading members of international café society.

One has an almost indelible image of Cole Porter absorbed in his work in the midst of treasure hunts, beach parties, fashionable outings and costume balls. Yet this fabulous, almost unreal world, which would seem on first blush to have a stifling effect on the development of his talent, actually sharpened his satiric gifts, enriched the quality of his art, and inspired some of his most original works.

Linda and Cole with Papuan chieftain, New Guinea, March, 1935

Yet the 1920's were filled with immense professional frustration for Cole as he was thought by many to be little more than a playboy-expatriate and succeeded in placing only a few songs in stage revues both in London and New York. Nevertheless, buoyed by the constant encouragement of Linda, he continued to work. It is no secret that the songs that seem to us to have been "tossed off" with the most casual effort were in fact the product of a lifelong dedication to his profession and nights and days of the most intense labor.

He worked away from the piano, writing the words and music almost simultaneously. First he created the opening and finish of a song, then proceeded from both beginning and ending toward the middle. The results often produced songs with a special artistic unity, fresh and unhackneyed, and free of many of the cliches of the vast preponderance of the songs of that age. Then, too, Porter was aloof from the mainstream of American life. Living in "exile" in Europe, he maintained some perspective on America's headlong pursuit of material utopia.

Finally, Porter's creative doldrums — the years of professional frustration after the failure of SEE AMERICA FIRST — ended when Monty Wooley asked him to submit songs for a Yale Dramat Christmas show in 1925. A visit to Venice by Fanny Brice in 1927 inspired some additional songs that were sung by Miss Brice at New York's Palace Theatre. Other songs were composed for friends and were performed at private parties. One song, I'm In Love Again, became a favorite of bandleaders after they heard it at Bricktop's in Paris and soon Paul Whiteman's recording made it a major success. But the most memorable assistance came from Irving Berlin, Porter's closest friend among theatre composers and a great admirer of Porter's work. He later wrote Cole that "Anything I can do, you can do better," while Porter thought Berlin to be America's best songwriter. Berlin suggested to Ray Goetz, his brother-in-law by a first marriage, that he persuade Cole to write some American songs with a French flavor for Goetz' new show PARIS. The show was to premiere at Berlin's Music Box Theatre in 1928 with Mrs. Goetz, the international favorite Irene Bordoni, in a starring role. The rest is theatrical history, as Let's Do It was a smash hit and from then on Porter's reputation was firmly established in the front ranks of the theatre.

At a recording session

The Porters attend an opening

Unlike the careers of the Gershwins, Rodgers and Hart, Vincent Youmans, DeSylva Brown and Henderson, and countless others, Cole's was no meteoric rise. He did not, as many of them did, come from the ranks of Tin Pan Alley via the traditional route of song plugger, rehearsal pianist, and vaudeville accompanist. His family wealth, while obviating the necessity of seeking this kind of employment, may have been a subtle barrier to his achievement.

With success Porter, in his own words, expanded like "a night-blooming flower." Shows such as *WAKE UP AND DREAM* (1929), *FIFTY MILLION FRENCHMEN* (1929), *THE NEW YORKERS* (1930), *GAY DIVORCE* (1932), *ANYTHING GOES* (1934) *JUBILEE* (1935), *RED HOT AND BLUE* (1936), *DuBARRY WAS A LADY* (1939), and countless others boasted numerous hit songs that buoyed the nation's spirits during the Depression. But it is not true that his most famous songs, *Night And Day* and *Begin The Beguine,* were failures when they were introduced. Nor is it true, as some allege, that Porter's creativity "dried up" after the tragic riding accident he suffered in October, 1937 which required over thirty operations and kept him in constant pain for the remainder of his life. A careful examination of the songs in this book reveals ample evidence of the continuing strength of his creativity.

Cole Porter died on October 15, 1964 and now, almost eight years after his death, we are in the midst of .what many people are calling a "Porter revival." Actually, while Porter's popularity has never waned, it is true that in the past few years his work has become more popular and more admired today than ever before. Hopefully, this volume will refresh the recollections of those who know and love his work and introduce thousands of others to the music and lyrics of a creator who shared his gifts with all of us, who challenged our intelligence, chronicled our foibles, and made us laugh and cry as he touched our hearts.

Mr. Kimball is the author of COLE, published by Holt, Rinehart & Winston.

LET'S DO IT

LET'S FALL IN LOVE

"Paris"

Words and Music by
COLE PORTER

12

Lith - u - an - i - ans and Letts do it,— Let's do it,—
Ev - en laz - y Jel - ly - fish do it,— Let's do it,—

Let's fall in — love.————— The Dutch in old Am - ster -
Let's fall in — love.————— E - lect - ric eels, I might —

dam do it,— Not to men - tion the Finns Folks in Si -
add, do it,— Though it shocks 'em I know. Why ask if —

14

LET'S DO IT

REFRAIN 2

The nightingales, in the dark, do it,
Larks, k-razy for a lark, do it,
Let's do it, let's fall in love.
Canaries, caged in the house, do it,
When they're out of season, grouse do it,
Let's do it, let's fall in love.
The most sedate barnyard fowls do it,
When a chantacleer cries,
High-browed old owls do it,
They're supposed to be wise,
Penguins in flocks, on the rocks, do it,
Even little cuckoos in their clocks, do it,
Let's do it, let's fall in love.

REFRAIN 4

The dragon flies, in the reeds, do it,
Sentimental centipedes do it,
Let's do it, let's fall in love.
Mosquitos, heaven forbid, do it,
So does ev'ry katydid, do it,
Let's do it, let's fall in love.
The most refined lady-bugs do it,
When a gentleman calls,
Moths in your rugs, do it,
What's the use of moth-balls?
Locusts in trees do it, bees do it,
Even highly educated fleas do it,
Let's do it, let's fall in love.

REFRAIN 5

The chimpanzees in the zoos do it,
Some courageous kangaroos do it,
Let's do it, let's fall in love.
I'm sure giraffes, on the sly, do it,
Heavy hippopotami do it,
Let's do it, let's fall in love.
Old sloths who hang down from twigs do it,
Though the effort is great,
Sweet guinea-pigs do it,
Buy a couple and wait.
The world admits bears in pits do it,
Even pekineses in the Ritz, do it,
Let's do it, let's fall in love.

Irene Bordoni, Arthur Margetson in PARIS (1928)

WHAT IS THIS THING CALLED LOVE?

"Wake Up And Dream"

Words and Music by
COLE PORTER

I was a hum-drum per-son, Lead-ing a life a- part, When love flew in through my win-dow wide And

17

LOVE FOR SALE

"The New Yorkers"

Words and Music by
COLE PORTER

NIGHT AND DAY

"Gay Divorce"

Words and Music by
COLE PORTER

26

27

Fred Astaire and Claire Luce in a scene from THE GAY DIVORCE (1932)

I GET A KICK OUT OF YOU

"Anything Goes"

Words and Music by
COLE PORTER

And I sud-den-ly turn and see _ your fab-u-lous face.

REFRAIN

I get no kick from cham - pagne, _____ Mere al-co-

hol does-n't thrill me at all, So tell me why should it be true. __

That I get a kick _ out of you? _____

YOU'RE THE TOP

VERSE 2

Your words poetic are not pathetic
On the other hand, boy, you shine
And I can feel after every line
A thrill divine
Down my spine.
Now gifted humans like Vincent Youmans
Might think that your song is bad,
But for a person who's just rehearsin'
Well I gotta say this my lad:

REFRAIN 3

You're the top!
You're a Ritz hot toddy.
You're the top!
You're a Brewster body.
You're the boats that glide on the sleepy Zuider Zee,
You're a Nathan panning,
You're a Bishop Manning,
You're broccoli.
You're a prize,
You're a night at Coney,
You're the eyes
Of Irene Bordoni.
I'm a broken doll, a fol-de-rol, a blop,
But if, Baby, I'm the bottom
You're the top!

REFRAIN 4

You're the top!
You're an Arrow collar.
You're the top!
You're a Coolidge dollar.
You're the nimble tread of the feet of Fred Astaire,
You're an O'Neill drama,
You're Whistler's mama,
You're Camembert.
You're a rose,
You're Inferno's Dante,
You're the nose
On the great Durante.
I'm just in the way, as the French would say
"De trop,"
But if, Baby, I'm the bottom
You're the top.

REFRAIN 5

You're the top!
You're a Waldorf salad.
You're the top!
You're a Berlin ballad.
You're a baby grand of a lady and a gent,
You're an old Dutch master,
You're Mrs. Astor,
You're Pepsodent.
You're romance,
You're the steppes of Russia,
You're the pants on a Roxy usher.
I'm a lazy lout that's just about to stop,
But if, Baby, I'm the bottom
You're the top.

REFRAIN 6

You're the top!
You're a dance in Bali.
You're the top!
You're a hot tamale.
You're an angel, you, simply too, too, too diveen,
You're a Botticelli,
You're Keats,
You're Shelley,
You're Ovaltine.
You're a boon,
You're the dam at Boulder,
You're the moon over Mae West's shoulder.
I'm a nominee of the G.O.P.
or GOP,
But if, Baby, I'm the bottom,
You're the top.

Ethel Merman, William Gaxton in ANYTHING GOES (1934)

REFRAIN 7

You're the top!
You're the Tower of Babel.
You're the top!
You're the Whitney Stable.
By the River Rhine,
You're a sturdy stein of beer,
You're a dress from Saks's,
You're next year's taxes,
You're stratosphere.
You're my thoist,
You're a Drumstick Lipstick,
You're da foist
In da Irish svipstick.
I'm a frightened frog
That can find no log
To hop,
But, if, Baby, I'm the bottom,
You're the top!

YOU'RE THE TOP

"Anything Goes"

Words and Music by
COLE PORTER

At words po-et-ic I'm so pa-thet-ic that I al-ways have found it best, In-stead of get-ting 'em off my chest, to let 'em rest un-ex-pressed. I hate pa-rad-ing my ser-e-nad-ing As I'll prob-a-bly miss a bar, But

36

ne Knight and Charles Walters dance BEGIN THE BEGUINE in JUBILEE (1935)

JUST ONE OF THOSE THINGS

"Jubilee"

Words and Music by
COLE PORTER

BEGIN THE BEGUINE

"Jubilee"

Words and Music by
COLE PORTER

44

I'VE GOT YOU UNDER MY SKIN

"Born To Dance"

Words and Music by
COLE PORTER

50

EASY TO LOVE

"Born To Dance"

Words and Music by
COLE PORTER

I know too well that I'm ___ just wast-ing pre - cious time in

think - ing such a thing could be, That you ___ could ev - er care for me,

Refrain (*slowly, with much expression*)

Original sheet music title page for BORN TO DANCE (1936)

GOODBYE, LITTLE DREAM, GOODBYE

"Red, Hot and Blue"

Words and Music by
COLE PORTER

DOWN IN THE DEPTHS
ON THE NINETIETH FLOOR

"Red, Hot and Blue"

Words and Music by
COLE PORTER

62

65

IT'S DE-LOVELY

"Red, Hot and Blue"

Words and Music by
COLE PORTER

HE
I feel a sud - den urge to sing,— The kind of dit - ty that in-

vokes the Spring,So con - trol your de - sire to curse while I cru - ci - fy the

68

69

✿ *Pronounced "delukes".*

IT'S DE-LOVELY

VERSE 2

She: Oh, charming sir, the way you sing
Would break the heart of Missus Crosby's Bing,
For the tone of your tra la la
Has that certain je ne sais quoi.
He: Oh, thank thee kindly, winsome wench,
But 'stead of falling into Berlitz French
Just warble to me, please,
This beautiful strain in plain Brooklynese.
She: Mi, mi, mi, mi,
Re, re, re, re,
Do, sol, mi, do, la, si
He: Take it away.

REFRAIN 2

Time marches on and soon it's plain
You've won my heart and I've lost my brain,
It's delightful, it's delicious, it's de-lovely.
Life seems so sweet that we decide
It's in the bag to get unified,
It's delightful, it's delicious, it's de-lovely.
See the crowd in that church,
See the proud parson plopped on his perch,
Get the sweet beat of that organ, sealing
our doom,
"Here goes the groom, boom!"
How they cheer and how they smile
As we go galloping down that aisle.
"It's divine, dear, it's diveen, dear,
It's de-wunderbar, it's de victory,
It's de vallop, it's de vinner, it's de voiks,
it's de-lovely."

REFRAIN 3

The knot is tied and so we take
A few hours off to eat wedding cake,
It's delightful, it's delicious, it's de-lovely.
It feels so fine to be a bride,
And how's the groom? Why, he's slightly fried,
It's delightful, it's delicious, it's de-lovely.
To the pop of champagne,
Off we hop in our plush little plane
Till a bright light through the darkness
cozily calls
"Niag'ra Falls."

All's well, my love, our day's complete,
And what a beautiful bridal suite,
"It's a d-reamy, it's de-rowsy,
It's de-reverie, it's de-rhapsody,
It's de-regal, it's de-royal, it's de-Ritz,
it's de-lovely."

REFRAIN 4

We settle down as man and wife
To solve the riddle called "married life,"
It's delightful, it's delicious, it's de-lovely.
We're on the crest, we have no cares,
We're just a couple of honey bears,
It's delightful, it's delicious, it's de-lovely.
All's as right as can be
Till, one night, at my window I see
An absurd bird with a bundle hung on his nose—
"Get baby clo'es."
Those eyes of yours are filled with joy
When Nurse appears and cries, "It's a boy,"
"He's appalling, he's appealing,
He's a polywog, he's a paragon,
He's a Pop-eye, he's a panic, he's a pip,
he's de-lovely."

REFRAIN 5

Our boy grows up, he's six feet, three,
He's so good looking, he looks like me,
It's delightful, it's delicious, it's de-lovely.
He's such a hit, this son of ours,
That all the dowagers send him flowers,
It's delightful, it's delicious, it's de-lovely.
So sublime is his press
That in time, L. B. Mayer, no less,
Makes a night flight to New York and tells him he should
Go Hollywood.
Good God!, today, he gets such pay
That Elaine Barrie's his fiancé,
"It's delightful, it's delicious,
"It's delectable, it's delirious,
"It's dilemma, it's delimit, it's deluxe, it's de-lovely."

Members of the cast: RED, HOT AND BLUE (1936)

RIDIN' HIGH

"Red, Hot and Blue"

Words and Music by
COLE PORTER

Love had socked me, sim-ply knocked me for ___ a loop.

Luck has dished me Till you fished me from ___ the soup.

74

RIDIN' HIGH

PATTER

What do I care
If Missus Harrison Williams is the best
    dressed woman in town?
What do I care
If Countess Barbara Hutton has a
    Rolls-Royce built for each gown?
Why should I have the vapors
When I read in the papers
That Missus Simpson dined behind
    the throne?
I've got a cute king of my own.
What do I care
If Katie Hepburn is famous for the world's
    most beautiful nose,
Or, if I, for my sins
Don't possess underpins

Like the pegs "Legs" Dietrich shows?
I'm feeling swell,
In fact so well
It's time some noise began,
For although I'm not
A big shot,
Still, I've got my man.

SECOND PATTER

What do I care
If Missus Dorothy Parker has the country's
    wittiest brain?
What do I care
If little Eleanor Jarrett only swims in
    vintage champagne?
Why should I be a-flutter

When Republicans mutter
That Missus R gets pay to write her day,
If I could write my nights, hey, hey!
What do I care
If fair Tallulah possesses tons and tons of
    jewels from gents?
Or, if some one observes
That I haven't the curves
That Simone Simon presents?
I'm doin' fine,
My life's divine,
I'm living in the sun
'Cause I've a big date
With my fate,
So I rate
A-1.

Sheet music cover for Cole's 1936 hit

OURS

PATTER

She: Don't say "Venice" to me,
    Or suggest that old Riviera,
    Those faded hot spots fill me with gloom, somehow,
    As for a Hindu temple, my pet,
    I wouldn't enter one on a bet.
    Why I'd be afraid of being chased by a sacred cow.
    Don't expect me to dream
    Of the silent Sierras, dear,
    Or to love that fattening cream
    That they give you in Devonshire,
    Don't mention the wilds of Paris,
    Or, as you call it "gay Paree,"
    I may not be right,
    But New York is quite
    Wild enough for me.

REFRAIN 2

She: Ours, the glitter of Broadway, Saturday night,
    Ours, a box at the Garden, watching a fight,
    Ours, the mad brouhaha of the Plaza's Persian Room,
    Or, if this fills you with gloom,
    We can go and admire Grant's tomb.
    Ours, a home on the river facing the East,
    Or on one of Park Avenue's least frightening tow'rs.
    All the chat you're chattin'
    Sounds to me like Latin,
    Why don't we stay in Manhattan
    And play it's all ours.

OURS

"Red, Hot and Blue"

Words and Music by
COLE PORTER

82

IN THE STILL OF THE NIGHT

"Rosalie"

Words and Music by
COLE PORTER

AT LONG LAST LOVE

"You Never Know"

Words and Music by
COLE PORTER

FROM ALPHA TO OMEGA

"You Never Know"

Words and Music by
COLE PORTER

93

94

Rex O'Malley, Clifton Webb, Lupe Velez, Libby Holman in YOU NEVER KNOW (1938)

FROM ALPHA TO OMEGA

REFRAIN 1

From Alpha to Omega,
From A to Z,
From Alpha to Omega,
You're made for me.
From left hooks by Dempsey to Braddock's upper-cuts,
From Jericho to Kokomo, not to mention from soup to nuts,
From Journal until Mirror,
From coast to coast,
From Juliet to Norma Shearer,
You're what I like the most,
And from morning until evening
In mis'ry I shall pine,
Till from Alpha to Omega you're mine.

REFRAIN 2

From Alpha to Omega,
From A to Z,
From Alpha to Omega,
You're made for me.
From love songs by Schumann to hits by Jerry Kern,
From Sarawak to Hackensack, not to mention,
    from stem to stern,
From dyah Missus Pat Campbell
To sweet Mae West,
You happen to be the mammal
This body loves the best,
And from morning until evening,
Will you stun yourself with wine?
Certainly, till from Alpha to Omega you're mine.

REFRAIN 3

From Alpha to Omega,
From A to Z,
From Alpha to Omega,
You're made for me.
From Lou Gehrig's home-run to Lou Chiozza's bunt,
From Tripoli to Kankakee, not to mention from
    Lynn to Lunt,
From great eighty-pound codfish
To sardines canned,
You happen to be the odd fish
This lad would love to land,
And will you woo me and pursue me,
With sinker, hook, and line?
Yes, till from Alpha to Omega you're mine.
And will you chase me,
And embrace me,
And say that I'm divine?
Till from Alpha to Omega you're mine.

REFRAIN 4

From Alpha to Omega,
From A to Z,
From Alpha to Omega,
You're made for me.
From cotton ploughed under
To this year's bumper crop,
From Benzedrine
To Ovaltine,
Not to mention from go to stop.
From corn muffins to Triscuit
From fat to thin,
From Zev to the young Seabiscuit,
I'll bet on you to win.
And will you brunch me,
And then lunch me,
Then make me stay to dine?
Yes, till from Alpha to Omega you're mine

REFRAIN 5

From Alpha to Omega,
From A to Z,
From Alpha to Omega,
You're made for me.
From old English Sherry
To very French Vermouth,
From Mozambique
To Battle Creek,
Not to mention from North to South.*
From great eagles to sparrows,
From large to small,
From Austins to big Pierce-Arrows,
Your rumble tops 'em all,
And will you beat me
And maltreat me,
And bend my Spanish spine?
Yes, till from Alpha to Omega you're mine.

*From COLE Note: Mr. Webb, go Southern,
and pronounce this Nauth and Sooth.

Finale
ACT II

From Martinis to brandy,
From East to West,
From Salomey to Sally Randy,
I like your fan the best,
And from morning until ev'ning,
The sun will never shine
Till from Alpha to Omega you're mine.

FAR AWAY

"Leave It To Me"

Words and Music by
COLE PORTER

Now that there is no ques-tion Of my not be-com-ing your wife,

I've a cer-tain sug-ges-tion As to our mar-ried life.

If you on-ly ac-cept it I shall prove my gra-ti-tude. Go

on, spring it, If pos-si-ble, sing it For I'm in a lyr-i-cal mood.

Refrain
Guitar tacet

1. I'm not sug-gest-ing to you   A draft-y cot-tage for
2. (I'm not sug)-gest-ing we get   A tent a-top of Thi-

two By the side of a wide wa-ter-fall,
bet, Or that we cross the sea in a yawl,

99

GET OUT OF TOWN

"Leave It To Me"

Words and Music by
COLE PORTER

Moderato

The farce was end - ed, The cur - tains drawn,

And I at least pre - tend - ed That love was dead and gone.

Close to me, dear,_ We touch too much._ The

thrill when we meet Is so bit-ter sweet That, dar-ling, it's get-ting me down.

So on your mark, get set, Get out of

town._____ town._____

MOST GENTLEMEN DONT LIKE LOVE

"Leave It To Me"

Words and Music by
COLE PORTER

109

MOST GENTLEMEN DON'T LIKE LOVE

REFRAIN 2

Most gentlemen don't like love, they just like
to kick it around,
Most gentlemen don't like love, 'cause most gentlemen
can't be profound.
So just remember when you get that glance,
A romp and a quickie
Is all little Dickie
Means
When he mentions romance,
For most gentlemen don't like love,
They just like to kick it around.

REFRAIN 3

Most gentlemen don't like love, they just like
to kick it around,
Most gentlemen don't like love, 'cause most gentlemen
can't be profound.
In ev'ry land, children, they're all the same,
A pounce in the clover
And then when it's over
"So long and what is your name?"
'Cause most gentlemen don't like love,
They just like to kick it around.

REFRAIN 4

Most gentlemen don't like love, they just like
to kick it around,
Most gentlemen don't like love, 'cause most gentlemen
can't be profound.
So if your boy friend, some fine night, should say
He'll love you forever
And part from you never,
Just push him out of the hay, (way)
'Cause most gentlemen don't like love,
They just like to kick it around.

Mary Martin sings MY HEART BELONGS TO DADDY as Gene Kelly and cast look on in LEAVE IT TO ME (1938)

MY HEART BELONGS TO DADDY

REFRAIN 2
Saint Patrick's day,
Although I may
Be seen wearing green with a paddy,
I'm always sharp
When playing the harp,
'Cause my heart belongs to Daddy.
Though other dames
At football games
May long for a strong undergraddy,
I never dream
Of making the team
'Cause my heart belongs to Daddy.
Yes, my heart belongs to Daddy,
So I simply couldn't be bad.
Yes, my heart belongs to Daddy,
Da-da, da-da-da, da-da-da, dad!
So I want to warn you, laddie,
Tho' I simply hate to be frank,
That I can't be mean to Daddy
'Cause my Da-da-da-daddy might spank.
In matters artistic
He's not modernistic
So Da-da-da-daddy might spank.

MY HEART BELONGS TO DADDY

"Leave It To Me"

Words and Music by
COLE PORTER

113

114

BETWEEN YOU AND ME

"Broadway Melody of 1940"

Words and Music by
COLE PORTER

Eleanor Powell and Fred Astaire dance the "Beguine" in the film BROADWAY MELODY OF 1940

I CONCENTRATE ON YOU

"Broadway Melody of 1940"

Words and Music by
COLE PORTER

BUT IN THE MORNING, NO

"DuBarry Was A Lady"

Words and Music by
COLE PORTER

Copyright © 1939 by Chappell & Co., Inc.
Copyright Renewed

128

BUT IN THE MORNING, NO

REFRAIN 2

He: Do you like the mountains, dear?
   Kindly tell me, if so.
She: Yes, I like the mountains, dear,
   But in the morning, no
He: Are you good at climbing, dear?
   Kindly tell me, if so.
She: Yes, I'm good at climbing, dear,
   But in the morning, no.
   When the light of the day
   Comes and drags me from the hay,
   That's the time
   When I'm
   In low.
He: Have you tried Pike's Peak, my dear?
   Kindly tell me, if so.
She: Yes, I've tried Pike's Peak, my dear,
   But in the morning, no, no—no, no,
   No, no, no, no, no!

REFRAIN 3

She: Are you fond of swimming, dear?
   Kindly tell me, if so.
He: Yes, I'm fond of swimming, dear,
   But in the morning, no.
She: Can you do the crawl, my dear?
   Kindly tell me, if so.
He: I can do the crawl, my dear,
   But in the morning, no.
   When the sun through the blind
   Starts to burn my poor behind
   That's the time
   When I'm
   In low.
She: Do you use the breast stroke, dear?
   Kindly tell me, if so.
He: Yes, I use the breast stroke, dear,
   But in the morning, no, no—no, no,
   No, no, no, no, no!

REFRAIN 4

He: Are you fond of Hot Springs, dear?
   Kindly tell me, if so.
She: Yes, I'm fond of Hot Springs, dear,
   But in the morning, no.
He: D'you like old Point Comfort, dear?
   Kindly tell me, if so.
She: I like old Point Comfort, dear,
   But in the morning, no.
   When my maid toddles in
   With my orange juice and gin,
   That's the time
   When I'm
   In low.
He: Do you like Mi-ami, dear?
   Kindly tell me, if so.
She: Yes, I like your-ami, dear,
   But in the morning, no, no—no, no,
   No, no, no, no, no!

NOTE: To satisfy the objections of some of the critics as well as the complaints of the Boston censors, Cole wrote the next two refrains:

REFRAIN 5

She: Are you good at football, dear?
   Kindly tell me, if so.
He: Yes, I'm good at football, dear,
   But in the morning, no.
She: Do you ever fumble, dear?
   Kindly tell me, if so.
He: No, I never fumble, dear,
   But in the morning, yes.
   When I start with a frown
   Reading Winchell upside down,
   That's the time
   When I'm
   In low.
She: Do you like a scrimmage, dear?
   Kindly tell me, if so.
He: Yes, I like a scrimmage, dear,
   But in the morning, no, no—no, no,
   No, no, no no, no!

REFRAIN 6

He: D'you like Nelson Eddy, dear?
   Kindly tell me, if so.
She: I like Nelson Eddy, dear,
   But in the morning, no.
He: D'you like Tommy Manville, dear?
   Kindly tell me, if so.
She: I like Tommy Manville, dear,
   But in the morning, no.
   When my maid says, "Madame!
   Wake 'em and make 'em scram,"
   That's the time
   When I'm
   In low.
He: Are you fond of Harvard men?
   Kindly tell me, if so.
She: Yes, I'm fond of Harvard men,
   But in the morning, no, no—no, no,
   No, no, no, no, no!

REFRAIN 7

She: Are you good at figures, dear?
   Kindly tell me, if so.
He: Yes, I'm good at figures dear,
   But in the morning, no.
She: D'you do double entry, dear?
   Kindly tell me, if so.
He: I do double entry, dear,
   But in the morning, no
   When the sun on the rise
   Shows the bags beneath my eyes.
   That's the time
   When I'm
   In low.
She: Are you fond of business, dear?
   Kindly tell me, if so.
He: Yes, I'm fond of business, dear,
   But in the morning, no, no—no, no,
   No, no, no, no, no!

REFRAIN 8

He: Are you in the market, dear?
   Kindly tell me, if so.
She: Yes, I'm in the market, dear,
   But in the morning, no.
He: Are you fond of bulls and bears?
   Kindly tell me, if so.
She: Yes, I'm fond of bears and bulls,
   But in the morning, no.
   When I'm waked by my fat
   Old canary, singing flat,
   That's the time
   When I'm
   In low.
He: Would you ever sell your seat?
   Kindly tell me, if so.
She: Yes, I'd gladly sell my seat,
   But in the morning, no, no—no, no,
   No, no, no, no, no!

REFRAIN 9

She: Are you fond of poker, dear?
   Kindly tell me, if so.
He: Yes, I'm fond of poker, dear,
   But in the morning, no.
She: Do you ante up, my dear?
   Kindly tell me, if so.
He: Yes, I ante up-my dear,
   But in the morning, no.
   When my old Gunga Din
   Brings the Bromo Seltzer in,
   That's the time
   When I'm
   In low.
She: Can you fill an inside straight?
   Kindly tell me, if so.
He: I've filled plenty inside straight,
   But in the morning, no, no—no, no,
   No, no, no, no, no!

REFRAIN 10

He: Are you fond of Democrats?
   Kindly tell me, if so.
She: Yes, I'm fond of Democrats,
   But in the morning, no.
He: Do you like Republicans?
   Kindly tell me, if so.
She: Yes, I like Republi-cans,
   But in the morning, no.
   When my pet pekinese
   Starts to cross his Q's and P's,
   That's the time
   When I'm
   In low.
He: Do you like third parties, dear?
   Kindly tell me, if so.
She: Yes, I love third parties, dear,
   But in the morning, no, no—no, no,
   No, no, no, no, no!

DO I LOVE YOU?

"DuBarry Was A Lady"

Words and Music by
COLE PORTER

KATIE WENT TO HAITI

"DuBarry Was A Lady"

Words and Music by
COLE PORTER

137

138

FRIENDSHIP

"DuBarry Was A Lady"

Words and Music by
COLE PORTER

141

KATIE WENT TO HAITI

REFRAIN 2

Katie stayed in Haiti
Spending all her pay.
Katie met a natie
Ev'ry other day.
Katie would tell the natie
That Katie was out for thrills
Each natie got a few for Katie
And Katie, she got the bills.
After a year in Haiti
She decided she should really go
But Katie had lived at such a ratie
That Katie had no dough
So Katie stuck to Haiti
Delighted with her fate
'Cause Katie still had Haiti
And practically all Haiti had Katie.

REFRAIN 3

Katie looked at Haiti
Feeling rather tired.
Katie met a natie
Katie was inspired.
After another natie
She sat down and wrote a book,
A guide-book for visitors to Haiti
Called "Listen, Stop, and Look!"
After the book by Katie
Had been published in the USA
The ratie of tourist trade in Haiti
Got bigger ev'ry day.
When Katie died at eighty
They buried her in state
For Katie made her Haiti
And practically all Haiti made Katie.

FRIENDSHIP

Cole Porter's original version

REFRAIN 1

He: If you're ever in a jam, here I am.
She: If you ever need a pal, I'm your gal.
He: If you ever feel so happy you land in jail,
   I'm your bail.
Both: It's friendship, friendship,
   Just a perfect blendship,
   When other friendships have been forgot,
   Ours will still be hot.
   Lahdle—ahdle——dig, dig, dig.

REFRAIN 2

She: If you ever lose your way, come to May.
He: If you ever make a flop, call for Pop.
She: If you ever take a boat and get lost at sea,
   Write to me.
Both: It's friendship, friendship,
   Just a perfect blendship.
   When other friendships have been forgit,
   Ours will still be it,
   Lahdle—ahdle—ahdle—chuck, chuck, chuck.

REFRAIN 3

He: If you're ever down a well, ring my bell.
She: If you ever catch on fire, send a wire.
He: If you ever lose your teeth and you're out to dine,
   Borrow mine.
Both: It's friendship, friendship,
   Just a perfect blendship,
   When other friendships have ceased to jell
   Ours will still be swell.
   Lahdle—ahdle—ahdle—hep, hep, hep.

REFRAIN 4

She: If they ever black your eyes, put me wise.
He: If they ever cook your goose, turn me loose.
She: If they ever put a bullet through your brr-ain,
   I'll complain.
Both: It's friendship, friendship,
   Just a perfect blendship.
   When other friendships go up in smoke
   Ours will still be oke.
   Lahdle—ahdle—ahdle—chuck, chuck, chuck.
   Gong, gong, gong,
   Cluck, cluck, cluck,
   Woof, woof, woof,
   Peck, peck, peck,
   Put, put, put,
   Hip, hip, hip.
   Quack, quack, quack,
   Tweet, tweet, tweet,
   Push, push, push,
   Give, give, give.

REFRAIN 5

He: If you ever lose your mind, I'll be kind.
She: If you ever lose your shirt, I'll be hurt.
He: If you're ever in a mill and get sawed in half,
   I won't laugh.
Both: It's friendship, friendship,
   Just a perfect blendship,
   When other friendships have been forgate,
   Ours will still be great.
   Lahdle—ahdle—ahdle—goof, goof, goof.

REFRAIN 6

She: If they ever hang you, pard, send a card.
He: If they ever cut your throat, write a note.
She: If they ever make a cannibal stew of you,
   Invite me too.
Both: It's friendship, friendship,
   Just a perfect blendship,
   When other friendships are up the crick,
   Ours will still be slick,
   Lahdle—ahdle—ahdle—zip, zip, zip.

WELL, DID YOU EVAH?

"DuBarry Was A Lady"

Words and Music by
COLE PORTER

WELL, DID YOU EVAH?

REFRAIN 1

She: Have you heard the coast of Maine
    Just got hit by a hurricane?
He: Well, did you evah! What a swell party this is.
She: Have you heard that poor, dear Blanche
    Got run down by an avalanche?
He: Well, did you evah! What a swell party this is.
    It's great, it's grand.
    It's Wonderland!
    It's tops, it's first.
    It's DuPont, it's Hearst!
    What soup, what fish.
    That meat, what a dish!
    What salad, what cheese!
She: Pardon me one moment, please,
    Have you heard that Uncle Newt
    Forgot to open his parachute?
He: Well, did you evah! What a swell party this is.
She: Old Aunt Susie just came back
    With her child and the child is black.
He: Well, did you evah! What a swell party this is.

REFRAIN 2

He: Have you heard it's in the stars
    Next July we collide with Mars?
She: Well, did you evah! What a swell party this is.
He: Have you heard that Grandma Doyle
    Thought the Flit was her mineral oil?
She: Well, did you evah! What a swell party this is.
    What Daiquiris!
    What Sherry! Please!
    What Burgundy!
    What great Pommery!
    What brandy, wow!
    What whiskey, here's how!
    What gin and what beer!
He: Will you sober up, my dear?
    Have you heard Professor Munch
    Ate his wife and divorced his lunch?
She: Well, did you evah! What a swell party this is.
He: Have you heard that Mimmsie Starr
    Just got pinched in the Astor Bar?
She: Well, did you evah! What a swell party this is!

REFRAIN 3

She: Have you heard that poor old Ted
    Just turned up in an oyster bed?
He: Well, did you evah! What a swell party this is.
She: Lilly Lane has louzy luck,
    She was there when the light'ning struck.
He: Well, did you evah! What a swell party this is.
    It's fun, it's fine,
    It's too divine.
    It's smooth, it's smart.
    It's Rodgers, it's Hart!
    What debs, what stags.
    What gossip, what gags!
    What feathers, what fuss!
She: Just between the two of us,
    Reggie's rather scatterbrained,
    He dove in when the pool was drained.
He: Well, did you evah! What a swell party this is.
She: Mrs. Smith in her new Hup
    Crossed the bridge when the bridge was up.
He: Well, did you evah! What a swell party this is!

He: Have you heard that Mrs. Cass
    Had three beers and then ate the glass?
She: Well, did you evah! What a swell party this is.
He: Have you heard that Captain Craig
    Breeds termites in his wooden leg?

Ethel Merman, Bert Lahr in DuBARRY WAS A LADY (1939)

She: Well, did you evah! What a swell party this is.
    It's fun, it's fresh.
    It's post depresh.
    It's Shangrilah.
    It's Harper's Bazaar!
    What clothes, quel chic,
    What pearls, they're the peak!
    What glamour, what cheer!
He: This will simply slay you dear,
    Kitty isn't paying calls,
    She slipped over Niagara Falls.
She: Well, did you evah! What a swell party this is.
He: Have you heard that Mayor Hague
    Just came down with bubonic plague?
She: Well, did you evah! What a swell party this is.

LET'S BE BUDDIES

"Panama Hattie"

Words and Music by
COLE PORTER

If you're on the town, If you're on your own, Well I'm sort a down and sick of be-ing a - lone, Do you ev-er spend your ev'nings with the blues? 'Cause if you do, my friend, we're both in the same shoes.

I'VE STILL GOT MY HEALTH

"Panama Hattie"

Words and Music by
COLE PORTER

I'VE STILL GOT MY HEALTH

REFRAIN 1

I'm always a flop at a top-notch affair,
But I've still got my health, so what do I care!
My best ring, alas, is a glass solitaire,
But I've still got my health, so what do I care!
By fashion and fopp'ry
I'm never discussed,
Attending the op'ry,
My box would be a bust!
When I give a tea, Lucius Beebe ain't there,
Well, I've still got my health, so what do I care!

VERSE 2

In spite of my Lux Movie skin
And Brewster body,
I've never joined the harem in
Scheherazade,
But, if so far, I've been a bust,
I'm stronger than the Bankers Trust
And you never have to give *this* one
Hunyadi.

REFRAIN 2

No rich Vanderbilt gives me gilt underwear,
But I've still got my health, so what do I care!
I've never been dined by refined L. B. Mayer,
But I've still got my health, so what do I care!
When Barrymore, he played
With his wife of yore,
The lead Missus B played,
But I played Barrymore,
She chased me a block for a lock of my hair,
Well, I've still got my health, so what do I care!

REFRAIN 3

I haven't the face of Her Grace, Ina Claire,
But I've still got my health, so what do I care!
I can't count my ribs, like His Nibs, Fred Astaire,
But I've still got my health, so what do I care!
Once I helped Jock Whitney
And as my reward,
I asked for a Jitney—
In other words, a Ford,
What I got from Jock was a sock, you know where,
Well, I've still got my health, so what do I care!

REFRAIN 4

When I'm in New York, I'm the Stork Club's despair,
But I've still got my health, so what do I care!
No radio chain wants my brain on the air,
But I've still got my health, so what do I care!
At school I was noted
For my lack of speed,
In fact I was voted
"Least likely to succeed,"
My wisecracks, I'm told are like old Camembert,
Well, I've still got my health, so what do I care!

VERSE 3

When Broadway first reviewed this wench,
The Press was catty,
They all agreed I'd even stench
In Cincinnati.
But, if I laid an awful egg,
I'm still as hot as Mayor Hague,
So in case you want to start a fire,
Wire Hattie.

REFRAIN 5

The hip that I shake doesn't make people stare,
But I've still got my health, so what do I care!
The sight of my props never stops thoroughfare,
But I've still got my health, so what do I care!
I knew I was slipping
At Minsky's one dawn,
When I started stripping,
They hollered "Put it on!"
Just once Billy Rose let me pose in the bare,
Well, I've still got my vitamins A, B, C, D,
E, F, G, H,
I
Still have my
Health.

Copyright © 1940 by Chappell & Co., Inc.
Copyright Renewed

Joan Carroll and Ethel Merman perform LET'S BE BUDDIES in PANAMA HATTIE (1940)

MAKE IT ANOTHER OLD FASHIONED, PLEASE

"Panama Hattie"

Words and Music by
COLE PORTER

162

make it an-oth-er Old Fash - ioned please!

Final ending please! please! Coda Leave out the

cher-ry Leave out the o - range! Leave out the

bit - ters! Just make it a straight rye!

SO NEAR AND YET SO FAR

You'll Never Get Rich

Words and Music by
COLE PORTER

Moderato

Piano

I so oft-en dream ____ We might make a team ____ But so

wild a scheme ____ I must ban-ish, For each

166

Rita Hayworth, Fred Astaire in the film musical YOU'LL NEVER GET RICH (1941)

EV'RYTHING I LOVE

"Let's Face It"

Words and Music by
COLE PORTER

173

FARMING

"Let's Face It"

Words and Music by
COLE PORTER

Here's a bit o' news that's quite a shock-er, Prov-ing Moth-er Na-ture still has charm,

Quot-ing Mis-ter Chol-ly Knick-er-bock-er "Get in the swim and buy a farm,"—

Jack Williams, Nanette Fabray, Danny Kaye, Sunnie O'Dea, and Benny Baker perform FARMING in LET'S FACE IT (1941)

REFRAIN 1

Farming, that's the fashion,
Farming, that the passion
Of our great celebrities of today.
Kit Cornell is shellin' peas,
Lady Mendl's climbin' trees,
Dear Mae West is at her best in the hay,
Stomping through the thickets,
Romping with the crickets,
Makes 'em feel more glamorous and more gay,
They tell me cows who are feeling milky
All give cream when they're milked by Willkie,
Farming is so charming, they all say.

REFRAIN 2

Farming, that's the fashion,
Farming, that's the passion
Of our great celebrities of today.
Monty Woolley, so I heard,
Has boll weevils in his beard,
Michael Strange has got the mange, will it stay?
Mussing up the clover,
Cussing when it's over,
Makes 'em feel more glamorous and more gay.
The natives think it's utterly utter
When Margie Hart starts churning her butter,
Farming is so charming, they all say.

REFRAIN 3

Farming, that's the fashion,
Farming, that's the passion
Of our great celebrities of today.
Fannie Hurst is haulin' logs,
Fannie Brice is feedin' hogs,
Garbo-Peep has led her sheep all astray,
Singing while they're rakin',
Bringing home the bacon,
Makes 'em feel more glamorous and more gay.
Miss Elsa Maxwell, so the folks tattle,
Got well-goosed while de-horning her cattle,
Farming is so charming, they all say.

REFRAIN 4

Farming that's the fashion,
Farming, that's the passion
Of our great celebrities of today.
Don't inquire of Georgie Raft
Why his cow has never calfed,
Georgia's bull is beautiful, but he's gay!
Seeing spring a-coming,
Being minus plumbing,
Makes 'em feel informal and dégagé.
When Cliff Odets found a new tomater
He ploughed under the Group Theaytre,
Farming is so charming, they all say.

REFRAIN 5

Farming, that's the fashion,
Farming, that's the passion,
Of our great celebrities of today.
Steinbeck's growing Grapes of Wrath,
Guy Lombardo, rumor hath,
Toots his horn and all the corn starts to sway,
Racing like the dickens,
Chasing after chickens,
Makes 'em feel more glamorous and more gay,
Liz Whitney has, on her bin of manure, a
Clip designed by the Duke of Verdura,
Farming is so charming, they all say.

(Among the discarded lines were the following:)

Farming, that's the fashion,
Farming, that's the passion
Of our great celebrities of today.
Digging in his fertile glen,
Goldwyn dug up Anna Sten,
Fred Astaire has raised a hare and its gray.
Clowning in their mittens,
Drowning extra kittens,
Makes 'em feel more glamorous and more gay.
Paul Whiteman, while he was puttin' up jelly,
Ate so much he recovered his belly,
Farming is so charming, they all say.

Farming, that's the fashion,
Farming, that's the passion,
Of our great celebrities of today
Missus Henry Morganthau
Looks so chic behind a plow,
Mrs. Hearst is at her worst on a dray.
Tearing after possum,
Wearing just a blossom,
Makes 'em feel more glamorous and more gay,
Why Orson Welles, that wonderful actor,
Has Del Rio driving a tractor.
Farming is so charming, they all say.

Farming, that's the fashion,
Farming, that's the passion,
Of our great celebrities of today.
Just to keep her roosters keen,
Dietrich that great movie queen,
Lifts her leg and lays an egg, what a lay.
Going after rabbits,
Knowing all their habits,
Makes 'em feel more glamorous and more gay.
So Harpo Marx, in a moment of folly,
Had his barn repainted by Dali.
Farming is so charming, they all say.

Farming, that's the fashion,
Farming, that's the passion,
Of our great celebrities of today.
Lynn Fontanne is brandin' steer,
Sophie Tucker, so I hear,
Rides en masse upon an ass, hip-hooray.
Hoeing new potatoes,
Throwing all tomatoes,
Makes 'em feel more glamorous and more gay.
So Clifton Webb has parked his Ma, Mabel,
"Way Down East" in a broken-down stable,
Farming is so charming, they all say.

LET'S NOT TALK ABOUT LOVE

REFRAIN 2

Let's talk about frogs, let's talk about toads,
Let's try to solve the riddle why chickens
    cross roads,
Let's talk about games, let's talk about sports,
Let's have a big debate about ladies in shorts,
Let's question the synonymy of freedom
    and autonomy,
Let's delve into astronomy, political economy,
Or if you're feeling biblical, the book
    of Deuteronomy,
But let's not talk about love.
Let's ride the New Deal, like Senator Glass,
Let's telephone to Ickes and order more gas,
Let's curse the Old Guard and Hamilton Fish,
Forgive me, dear, if Fish is your favorite dish,
Let's heap some hot profanities on Hitler's
    inhumanities,
Let's argue if insanity's the cause of
    his inanities,
Let's weigh the Shubert Follies with The Ear-rl
    Carroll Vanities,
But let's not talk about love.
Let's talk about drugs, let's talk about dope,
Let's try to picture Paramount minus Bob Hope,
Let's start a new dance, let's try a new step,
Or investigate the cause of Missus Roosevelt's pep,
Why not discus, my dee-arie,
The life of Wallace Bee-ery
Or bring a jeroboam on
And write a drunken poem on
Astrology, mythology,
Geology, philology,
Pathology, psychology,
Electro-physiology,
Spermology, phrenology,
I owe you an apology
But let's not talk about love.

REFRAIN 3

Let's speak of Lamarr, the Hedy so fair,
Why does she let Joan Bennett wear all
    her old hair?
If you know Garbo, then tell me this news,
Is it a fact the Navy's launched all
    her old shoes?
Let's check on the veracity of Barrymore's
    bibacity
And why his drink capacity should get so
    much publacity,
Let's even have a huddle over Ha'vard
    Univassity,
But let's not talk about love.
Let's wish him good luck, let's wish him
    more pow'r,
That Fiorella fella, my favorite flow'r,
Let's get some champagne from over
    the seas,
And drink to Sammy Goldwyn,
Include me out please.
Let's write a tune that's playable,
    a ditty swing-and-swayable
Or say whatever's sayable, about the
    Tow'r of Ba-abel,
Let's cheer for the career of itty-bitty
    Betty Gra-abel,
But let's not talk about love.
In case you play cards, I've got some
    right here
So how about a game o' gin-rummy, my dear?
Or if you feel warm and bathin's your whim,
Let's get in the all-together and
    enjoy a short swim,
No honey, Ah suspect you all
Of bein' intellectual
And so, instead of gushin' on,
Let's have a big discussion on
Timidity, stupidity, solidity, frigidity,
Avidity, turbidity, Manhattan, and viscidity,
Fatality, morality, legality, finality,
Neutrality, reality, or Southern hospitality,
Pomposity, verbosity,
You're losing your velocity
But let's not talk about love.

LET'S NOT TALK ABOUT LOVE

"Let's Face It"

Words and Music by
COLE PORTER

have a big de-bate a-bout la-dies in shorts, Let's check on the ve-ra-ci-ty of

Bar-ry-more's bi-ba-ci-ty And why his drink ca-pa-ci-ty should get so much pub-la-ci-ty, Let's

e-ven have a hud-dle o-ver Ha'-vard U-ni-va-si-ty, But let's not talk a-bout

love   Let's wish him good luck, Let's wish him more pow'r That Fi-o-rel-la fel-la, my

184

185

I HATE YOU, DARLING

"Let's Face It"

Words and Music by
COLE PORTER

YOU'D BE SO NICE TO COME HOME TO

"Something To Shout About"

Words and Music by
COLE PORTER

COULD IT BE YOU

"Something For The Boys"

Words and Music by
COLE PORTER

I LOVE YOU

"Mexican Hayride"

Words and Music by
COLE PORTER

198

EV'RY TIME WE SAY GOODBYE

"Seven Lively Arts"

Words and Music by
COLE PORTER

Original sheet music cover designs

1942

1944

1944

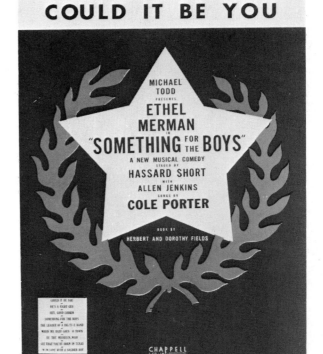

1943

USE YOUR IMAGINATION

"Out Of This World"

Words and Music by
COLE PORTER

FROM THIS MOMENT ON

"Out Of This World"

Words and Music by
COLE PORTER

213

I AM LOVED

"Out Of This World"

Words and Music by
COLE PORTER

Moderato (*Slow Fox-trot tempo*)

Yes - ter - day _____ was a dull day, _____

Yes - ter - day _____ was a gray day, _____ But

WHERE, OH WHERE

"Out Of This World"

Words and Music by
COLE PORTER

227

Original sheet music cover for OUT OF THIS WORLD

Playbill for OUT OF THIS WORLD which opened Dec. 21, 1950 starring Charlotte Greenwood

YOU DON'T REMIND ME

"Out Of This World"

Words and Music by
COLE PORTER

IT'S ALL RIGHT WITH ME

"Can-Can"

Words and Music by
COLE PORTER

Steadily moving fox trot

Refrain

It's the wrong time ____ and the wrong place ____ tho' your

face is charm - ing, it's the wrong face, ____ it's not

{her}
{his} face ____ but such a charm - ing face ____ that it's

238

I LOVE PARIS

"Can-Can"

Words and Music by
COLE PORTER

ALLEZ-VOUS-EN, GO AWAY

"Can - Can"

Words and Music by
COLE PORTER

245

*Pronounce: Al-lay-voo-zon
(French for Go away.)

C'EST MAGNIFIQUE

"Can-Can"

Words and Music by
COLE PORTER

*Pronounced "say man-yee-fee-kuh"

C'EST MAGNIFIQUE

VERSE 2

Aristide: When you began of love to speak,
I followed every word.
But when you called love magnifique,
I would have called it absurd
And when you said it was often tragique,
I would have said it was always comique.
So, mad'moiselle, be sweet to me
And kindly do not repeat to me.

Copyright © 1952 & 1953 by
Chappell & Co., Inc.

Shubert Theatre program cover for CAN-CAN (892 performances)

STEREOPHONIC SOUND

"Silk Stockings"

Words and Music by
COLE PORTER

255

Pronounce "zound"

Ab   **Db**   **Ab**

wide, You've got— to have glo-ri-ous tech-ni-col-or, Breath-tak-ing
care Un-less— she had glo-ri-ous tech-ni-col-or, Breath-tak-ing

Dbm   **1. Ab**   **Dbm**   **Ab**

cin-e-ma-scope or Cin-e-ra-ma, Vis-ta-vi-sion, Su-per-scope or
cin-e-ma-scope or

mf sub.

Dbm   **Ab**   **C+**   **F7**

**Tod-da-o and Ste-re-o-phon-ic sound,_____ and

cresc.   *ff*   *f*

Bb9   **Eb7(b9)**   **Ab**   **Eb7**   **Eb+**

Ste-re-o-phon-ic sound._____   You

ff   *mf*

**Pronounce "Tod-day-o"

AS ON THROUGH THE SEASONS WE SAIL

"Silk Stockings"

Words and Music by
COLE PORTER

261

ALL OF YOU

"Silk Stockings"

Words and Music by
COLE PORTER

Fox trot tempo

Piano

mf

Bb7

(with bounce, but not too fast)

Eb

mp

Af - ter watch-ing her ap - peal from ev - 'ry an - gle,

Bb7

There's a big ro - man - tic deal I've got to

Eb

Fm

wan - gle. For I've fal - len for a

266

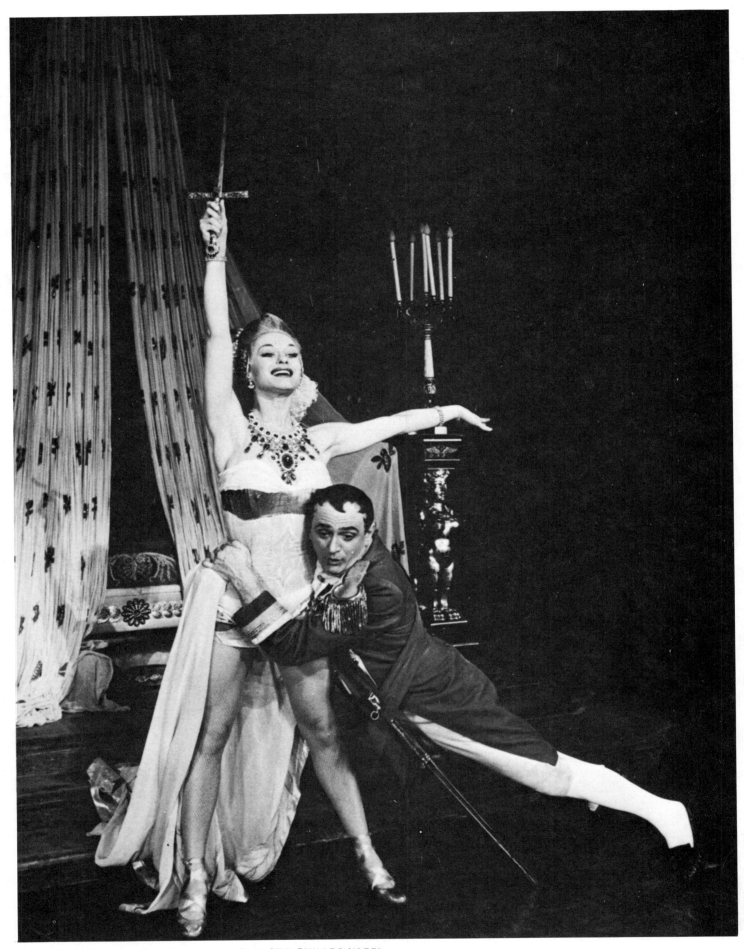

Gretchen Wyler, Stanley Simmons in SILK STOCKINGS (1955)

TRUE LOVE

"High Society"

Words and Music by
COLE PORTER

MIND IF I MAKE LOVE TO YOU

"High Society"

Words and Music by
COLE PORTER

YOU'RE SENSATIONAL

"High Society"

Words and Music by
COLE PORTER

He: A thor-ough know-ledge I've got a-bout girls, I've been a round__
She: A thor-ough know-ledge I've got a-bout boys, I've been a round__

And af-ter learn-ing a lot a-bout__ girls,
And af-ter learn-ing a lot a-bout__ boys,

This is the im-port-ant fact I found:
This is the im-port-ant fact I found:

Frank Sinatra, Grace Kelly in HIGH SOCIETY (1956)

Mitzi Gaynor, Kay Kendall, Taina Elg in LES GIRLS (1957)

ÇA, C'EST L'AMOUR

"Les Girls"

Words and Music by
COLE PORTER

WOULDN'T IT BE FUN

"Aladdin"

Words and Music by
COLE PORTER

SHOW-FILM CHRONOLOGY

A listing of the 58 songs contained in this book, the shows from which they came, and the artists who introduced them